Keto for Comfort Eaters

Paula Willis

Published by Paula Willis, 2023.

While every precaution has been taken in the preparation of this book, the publisher assumes no responsibility for errors or omissions, or for damages resulting from the use of the information contained herein.

KETO FOR COMFORT EATERS

First edition. October 21, 2023.

ISBN: 979-8223829133

Written by Paula Willis.

Table of Contents

For those of us who needed to find comfort in food, may we not need comfort to soothe our souls because we are enough already.

Be kind to yourself, you've already got this! x

Keto for Comfort Eaters - Reclaiming Control Over Emotional Eating

1

Introduction

Depending on food for emotional peace and happiness is a struggle many people go through. It makes you feel out of control, and despite its name, comfort food doesn't end up being all that comforting!

If you feel like you've tried everything and are at the end of your tether, you're not alone. Recovery from comfort eating is hard, but it is possible.

That's where the ketogenic diet or "keto" comes in.

Backed by scientific research and the real-life experiences of many ex-comfort eaters, keto can help you stop emotional eating once and for all.

I'm not saying this journey will be easy - changing habits and freeing yourself from unhelpful habits never is, but together, we're going to harness the power of the keto diet so you can finally find food freedom.

Understanding the Psychology of Comfort Eating

UNDERSTANDING THE REASONS why you eat emotionally is complex. You may have many underlying triggers, deep-rooted negative self-beliefs or feel out of control in your life. This book is all about taking those first steps to food freedom.

We'll look at identifying your triggers, learning to forgive yourself and setting better habits in place through the keto diet to move away from comfort eating and break free of the constricting feelings caused by emotional eating.

The Promise of Keto: A Path to Freedom from

Emotional Eating

FINDING YOUR WAY TO freedom from emotional eating is a tricky path filled with trial and error. Keto has been found to help those suffering from emotional eating break the cycle and learn to stop using food to resolve emotional distress.

With keto, not only will you take back control of your eating, but you'll also be able to lose some of the weight you may have gained as a result of your unhealthy relationship with food.

This journey isn't about judging you or your body. It's about accepting where you are today and moving forward in a way that supports your mental and physical health.

So embrace the wild ride, and let's get ready to heal your relationship with food through keto!

Chapter 1: Unmasking Comfort Eating

Recognizing the Triggers: Stress, Anxiety and Depression

Comfort eating has nothing to do with food and hunger. Emotional eating is your brain's attempt to self-soothe to avoid the nasty feelings that wash over you when you feel emotionally uncomfortable. That includes times of stress, anxiety, depression and even boredom.

Have you ever felt anxious about something, felt a physical nervous sensation in your stomach and immediately reached for a chocolate bar to remove that feeling? **That's emotional eating**. The issue is, that it's pretty hard to recognize when you're eating to control your emotions and when you're eating for hunger because, in both situations, you likely feel an empty sensation in your stomach.

That's why the very first step on the journey to recovery is to understand what's causing your emotional discomfort and the situations that trigger comfort eating for you.

Decoding Your Emotional Connection with Food

THE TRICKY THING ABOUT emotional eating is that you often second-guess yourself. Your psychological triggers can quickly feel like hunger cues, leading you to doubt whether you actually need to eat or not.

Harder still, there's not just one universal pattern or cause of emotional eating. In fact, over the years, scientists have come up with a wide range of theories as to why emotional eating happens.

It all starts with meeting your basic needs. According to Timmerman and Acton (2001), people who can't satisfy their basic psychological needs are more likely to use emotional eating as a coping mechanism. It becomes an act of self-soothing.

Macht (2008) takes this theory even further, giving a five-way model that outlines the five most common ways emotions interact with eating. Most people will identify more strongly with one or two of these categories. Take a look at the five categories and see which one (or two) you resonate most with.

1. Emotion-driven food choice

FOR EACH NEGATIVE EMOTION, you have a specific go-to comfort food to help self-soothe. For example, when you're feeling stressed at work, you may specifically grab a packet of crisps to eat to calm down. Often, these foods are high in sugar and fat, which ultimately leave you feeling worse in the long run.

2. Emotion-induced eating

EMOTIONAL DISTRESS and discomfort trigger comfort eating as a way of dealing with negative body sensations and shifting your focus away from your feelings. What follows is usually overeating to physically fill the empty sensation in your stomach created by your emotional needs not being met. This is the most common and most well-known version of emotional eating.

3. Emotion-enhanced taste perception

OUR EMOTIONS CAN INFLUENCE our taste buds, making foods taste better during heightened emotions. This is what makes comfort foods taste even better during emotional distress and why you're more likely to reach for certain foods when you're stressed, anxious, or depressed. So if, on your average day, you wouldn't typically think about eating biscuits, but during high emotional situations, you strongly crave them, your comfort eating likely falls into this bracket.

4. Emotion-induced food aversion

IN THE SAME WAY, SOME foods taste better when you're emotional, you may find yourself completely put off by others. This helps solidify the idea of comfort foods and is why we tend to indulge in "safe foods" that make us feel better. For example, when you're feeling scared or anxious, you may find that your delicious plate of oven-roasted vegetables suddenly puts you off and makes you feel nauseous.

5. Emotional regulation

FINALLY, FOOD MAY BECOME a coping mechanism within itself, where you reach for your favourite comfort foods to avoid emotional discomfort before it comes or to make yourself feel happy when you feel down. In this case, comfort food is used more as a preventative medicine or supplement rather than a response to a specific situation.

Understanding which category you fall into will make understanding your comfort eating behaviour patterns easier. And once you spot the pattern, you're halfway to success.

Thanks to advancements in neuroimaging, we can now see the physical effect comfort food has on our brain, giving us a fuller picture of the processes that help solidify a pattern of emotional eating. According to Godet et al. (2022), when we comfort eat, the parts of the brain associated with reward and the parts related to emotional regulation are both activated. This shows the importance of a multiple-discipline approach where we understand the need for fulfilment as well as emotional regulation in overcoming comfort eating. That means when dealing with your comfort eating, you need to find things that make you feel happy and alive while also finding the right emotional support for your mental wellbeing so you don't resort to food as a coping mechanism.

Interestingly, the extent to which our choices in comfort food are actually comforting varies from person to person. Van Strien et al. (2019) found that although comfort food can provide some emotional relief, it heavily depends on the person and situation. In many cases, there is a tendency to reach for certain foods (like chocolate or french fries) out of habit, but the short-lived dopamine release doesn't do much to hide the underlying distress.

Understanding the science behind comfort eating is a good first step, but it only gives part of the picture. It's easy to understand that your emotions are driving your eating habits, but it's much harder to pinpoint what is triggering this behaviour. To understand what's going on in your own mind and the unique patterns that cause you to emotionally eat.

To help you start to decode your underlying emotional eating triggers, asking yourself questions is the best course of action. It's a powerful tool for uncovering your unique emotional patterns and comfort eating triggers so you can find the root sources of your emotional eating.

I have added five self-assessment questionnaires at the back of this book to help get you started. Really take your time to think about your answers and try to give as much detail as possible. No one will read this except you, so allow yourself to be as vulnerable as you can be. And if you feel overwhelmed, remember you don't have to do these assessments all at once; you can do them on different days or keep coming back to them if you need to.

Make sure to keep your answers safe and refer back to them often. These answers will help you unlock the key to understanding why you comfort eat. And once you start to notice the patterns, you can make a plan to start breaking them.

The Revolving Door of Comfort Eating

NOTICING YOUR EMOTIONAL discomfort and comfort eating patterns is an important first step in your recovery. But knowing it's happening doesn't solve the problem on its own.

Many studies suggest our typical go-to comfort foods release dopamine into our bodies. Dopamine is the feel-good hormone that lights up our brain's reward centre to reinforce certain behaviours. It's why it's so easy to binge-watch Netflix — the more we get a hit of dopamine, the more likely we are to repeat the action in search of even more dopamine to make us feel happy and fulfilled.

The problem is dopamine doesn't discriminate based on action. If it's fun or makes you happy, you'll get a dopamine release. So simply telling yourself, "Oh, I know I'm eating because I'm feeling emotionally uncomfortable", isn't enough to stop the dopamine release.

Instead, you need to find ways to deal with your emotions head-on and replace the comfort eating habit with behaviours that make you feel good while also being good *for you*.

The way you do this will be unique to your situation. It can be anything from talking to friends or journaling to seeking professional help from a licensed therapist. Look for activities that make you feel grounded, safe and happy. Some of the most popular activities for emotional regulation include:

- Mindfulness

- Deep breathing

- Movement or exercise

- Journaling

- Art and creative expression (writing, painting, knitting, singing, pottery, etc.)

- Hanging out with friends

- Massages or spa days for muscle relaxation

- Talking to a therapist

- Connecting with nature through outdoor activities

- Listening to music

- Hanging out with friends

Once you start dealing with your uncomfortable emotions and finding the root cause, you've begun the important path to food freedom. Alongside your non-food coping activities for emotional discomfort, it's time to replace those high-sugar foods that make you feel drained and perpetuate your negative emotions with more nourishing options that support your mental health healing.

That's where keto comes in.

Chapter 2: The Keto Lifestyle

What is the Keto Diet?

Keto may sound like one of those scary diets where you have to give up your entire life to make it work, but it's far simpler than you think. Personally, I don't like to think of it as a diet; I prefer to see it as a lifestyle change. It's not about being overly restrictive to punish yourself, as is the case with many other diets. Instead, it's about adding more of certain types of food to your daily menu to feel physically and mentally healthier.

Essentially, a keto diet aims to control the proportions of the three main macronutrients you consume — carbohydrates, proteins and fats — to allow the body to go into ketosis. For the keto diet, your aim is for your daily macronutrient intake to be approximately 70%-80% healthy fats, 10%-20% proteins and 5%-10% carbohydrates.

Keto is a popular tool for dealing with emotional eating for a reason.

One of the major side effects of comfort eating is weight gain. This is particularly true for people who frequently overeat high-fat and sugar foods with many calories as a coping mechanism for their emotions. And if overeating has caused you to gain weight, that weight may make you feel self-conscious or otherwise exacerbate your emotional distress. As such, for many people, losing weight is a goal that comes alongside emotional eating. But if you're already suffering from disordered eating and haven't addressed the fundamental core of why it's happening, then following a diet where you're restricting calories can make your comfort eating worse, potentially even developing a binge eating disorder as a result.

By using keto as a tool to regain control of your emotional eating, you may find you're able to lose weight without triggering any disordered eating.

While keto can be a useful tool for weight loss, this doesn't need to be your goal. In fact, whether or not you want to lose weight will depend a lot on how many calories you're eating just as much as the type of food you're eating, so if you're not interested in weight loss or calorie counting, this is not a necessary part of this lifestyle. There are many other reasons and health benefits to be gained on a keto diet. These include:

- Managing Diabetes
- Reducing Stress
- Reducing blood pressure
- Improve cholesterol levels
- Managing blood glucose levels
- Improving satiety (hunger) levels
- Reducing the recurrence of thrush and yeast infections

It's important to note that not all keto diets are created equal. To get the benefits of the keto diet, you still need to ensure you're focusing on getting minimally processed foods as opposed to ultra-processed foods, as these can have physical and mental negative health effects.

For example, some artificial sweeteners are known to exacerbate mental health problems, including emotional eating or its evolved state, binge eating disorder.

Beyond the Scale: Keto's Benefits on Your Mental Health and Emotional Stability

WHEN WE THINK OF MENTAL health, we think of the mind and the brain. But an equally important connection is often overlooked — **the gut-brain connection.**

Our guts are known as the second brain because many of our hormones are created as neurochemicals released by gut bacteria. Serotonin is an excellent example of this, with 95% of the body's supply of serotonin being created in the gut.

One of the main reasons keto helps with emotional stability is that it improves your gut biome, essentially healing or improving your gut-brain health. With diets higher in carbohydrates, the sugars ingested can cause a disturbance to your natural gut biome, leading to an imbalance. As well as some uncomfortable physical symptoms such as bloating and flatulence, it also disrupts the creation and release of essential neurochemicals that aid mental wellness and balance.

The great thing about keto is it is naturally low in sugar, meaning far less disruption to the biome. However, as I mentioned before, this also relies on having a keto diet that is mostly minimally processed, as ultra-processed foods tend to contain chemical compounds that disrupt the bacteria inside your gut.

Keto as a Tool for Taming Your Triggers

BALANCING YOUR GUT biome is an essential way that keto reduces the urge to comfort eat. But it's not the only way. Have you ever heard the expression "out of sight, out of mind"? When we reach for comfort food, it's usually high sugar and high carb (think chocolate, pastries, pizza, ice cream, fries, etc.). While the science is still developing, some experts believe sugar can become addictive, so the more you eat it, the more you crave it. With keto, these foods aren't on the table, so you'll be less likely to pick them up. And with decreased sugars and carbs come fewer insulin spikes, which in turn means more stable blood glucose levels and helps combat cravings.

It's important to note that just because sugar is off the keto menu doesn't mean your cravings will disappear when you embark on your keto journey. As with every lifestyle change, it will take some time to train your body to stop craving these foods as an emotional blanket, but as you'll see in Chapter 3, I've outlined the perfect keto toolkit for you to empower your journey and help you feel confident in not only starting but also continuing to follow a keto lifestyle.

Chapter 3: Getting Started with Keto

The Basics of Ketosis

As discussed earlier, the body needs three key macronutrients to survive - carbohydrates, healthy fats, and proteins. The body has a specific order of burning these nutrients to create energy for the body. Specifically, our bodies almost always burn carbohydrates first, so we can use glucose as our main energy source. This is because it is much easier and quicker for the body to break down glucose into energy than it is to break down fats.

Limiting the amount of carbohydrates you consume means your body can no longer rely on carbohydrates for energy and instead move on to fats. This is the foundation of ketosis.

Ketosis is the process in which the body burns fats, producing an acid called ketones, which is then used for energy around the body. When you follow a ketogenic diet, your body has too few carbohydrates in the body to use as energy, encouraging it to use fat for energy instead and saving the carbohydrates for other essential bodily needs.

Of course, following a generic macronutrient breakdown is not enough to ensure your body is in ketosis. Everybody is unique, and consequently, every keto threshold (that is, the macronutrient breakdown needed to keep your body in ketosis) is different. To test whether or not your body is in ketosis, you should use ketone urine test strips or ketone blood-prick tests. These are easily found in pharmacies or online, and are essential for monitoring your ketone levels to understand if your body is in ketosis. It will also act as a good guide to your optimal keto diet proportions and whether or not you need to continue adjusting your food plan.

For ketosis to work, you need to constantly stay below a certain carbohydrate threshold. This threshold differs between individuals but is typically around 10% carbohydrate intake. It may be tempting to cut carbohydrates out of your diet completely, but this is extremely dangerous. While you are aiming to get your energy from healthy fats, carbohydrates still play a vital role in your physical health, and cutting them out completely can lead to some serious health complications. That's why it's crucial to only cut down to as much as you need to to reach ketosis and no more.

Once you find your ketosis macronutrient breakdown, you must be careful not to exceed your carbohydrate load. If you eat too many carbohydrates, your body may "kick you out" of ketosis, and you'll have to start the process again. Luckily, the longer your body is in ketosis, the easier and quicker it is to get back into it. But you may still suffer the same side effects (see below) as you did when starting the keto journey in the first place, which is not very pleasant.

The keto diet can be life-changing for your health goals. For example, this lifestyle can help you lose weight in a way not many other eating plans can. It reduces your insulin spikes, giving you more energy throughout the day without those dreaded crashes. The reduction of blood sugars also explains why keto is so successful at managing diabetes and high blood pressure in many patients.

However, as is life, with the good also comes the bad, and keto does have some side effects you should be aware of before deciding to start the keto lifestyle.

The first downside of ketosis comes within the first few weeks when many participants often report what is commonly referred to as the "keto flu." As your body adapts to this new way of functioning, you may experience symptoms such as nausea, fatigue, constipation, sleep disturbance and headaches. It's a normal response to a significant diet change; experts say the keto flu doesn't last more than two weeks. Still, it can be uncomfortable and may make life harder for a few weeks, so you'll need to plan around this possibility (especially if you have any important events coming up soon).

Another potential side effect to be aware of is "keto breath." As your body enters ketosis, your breath might start to smell fruity or even like nail polish — all thanks to the chemicals produced during the process. This is also a temporary symptom and should subside within a few months of starting the diet.

Finally, there is a small risk of diabetic ketoacidosis, where ketones build up in the blood. This is a serious condition, so if you have diabetes, it's essential to seek medical advice before starting a keto diet.

As with every lifestyle change, it's always best to consult a doctor before starting, and this is especially true for those with underlying illnesses, those worried about their health and those who are pregnant, breastfeeding or trying to conceive.

Building your Keto Toolkit

NOW WE'VE GOT THE SCIENCE out of the way; it's time to get excited by building your keto toolkit. Planning is the number one way to guarantee your success and to prepare yourself to succeed against falling back into your emotional eating habits.

Here's everything you need to set yourself up for success:

1. Keto food list

FOLLOWING A KETO LIFESTYLE can be pretty daunting at first glance. Suddenly, there are a bunch of foods you're used to eating that don't fit your new lifestyle. So having a list of keto-friendly foods is going to help make grocery shopping and meal prepping a whole lot easier. Keep multiple copies around the house where you'll see them when you need them. Post one on your fridge, keep a digital copy in your phone's notes app and put it in your food cupboard.

2. Keto recipe collection

ONE OF THE EASIEST ways to be prepared for the keto lifestyle is to have a go-to pack of keto recipes you can rely on. Choose recipes that are satisfying, delicious and make you feel great.

If you're not the best home cook, think of this as your opportunity to start building skills in the kitchen. Start easy and build from there. Over time, as you keep finding new recipes you love, your recipe index will grow, and before you know it, you'll be swimming in keto recipe ideas!

3. Keto test strips

AS I MENTIONED EARLIER, the only way to tell if your body is in ketosis is to test it by using either ketone urine test strips or ketone blood-prick tests. To make life easier when you begin your keto lifestyle, ensure you have a good supply so you don't run out. At the beginning of your keto journey, you'll want to monitor your ketone levels at least once a day to ensure you're in ketosis. As you'll only know your body's optimal carbohydrate intake for ketosis through trial and error, using ketone test strips will help you track if you're eating too many carbohydrates so you can adjust accordingly.

4. Meal prepping equipment

FOLLOWING THE KETO lifestyle is all about choosing whole foods or minimally processed foods that kick you into ketosis to yield some pretty impressive physical and mental health improvements. But let's be honest; not everyone has the time to cook a hearty meal three to five times a day. That's why meal prepping is a game changer when following the keto diet.

Make sure you have plenty of Tupperware available to stock up on meals and make space in your freezer to store it all.

And if you want to go even further, I'd highly recommend investing in a good slow cooker for easy, no-fuss, one-pot meals that can easily be bulk-cooked with low effort.

5. A list of keto-friendly meal kits and takeaway places

IF YOU WANT TO EMBRACE the keto lifestyle truly, then it's important to be realistic about your journey. While cooking from scratch is great and full of benefits, you won't always have the time for it. And let's be honest, sometimes you just can't be bothered to cook and want a delicious takeaway to indulge in.

Having a list of go-to restaurants, takeaway menus, and DIY meal kits will save you a headache when you only want to lie on the sofa, chill out with Netflix and let someone else deal with your food for the night.

Remember, your toolkit is about being realistic, not perfect.

6. Food journal

WHEN TRYING TO BREAK free of the chains of emotional eating, you need a place to reflect on your progress. And when you add a new keto diet to the equation, you need a way to determine whether your symptoms are improving.

Your food journal should track:

- What you're eating

- The time you're eating

- Your mood before you eat

- Any emotional triggers you had before you ate (stress, boredom, anxiety, depression, etc.)

- Did you enjoy your meal? What about it did you enjoy?

- How hungry you felt before you ate

- How full/satisfied you felt after you ate

This journal serves two purposes. The first is to help you spot patterns between your triggers and your eating habits. Do you reach for food after a stressful Zoom meeting with your boss? Do you suddenly feel hungry when you've been sitting on your sofa for hours trying to find something to watch on TV? Everyone has different triggers that cause emotional eating. But it's not until you track your eating habits that you can truly see the patterns that cause it so you can work on breaking them.

The second purpose is to track your keto diet and how it makes you feel, allowing you to find the foods that make you feel great.

With the keto diet, you may find that as your meals make you feel more satisfied and your blood sugar levels stop spiking as much, your triggers do not lead you to eat as often.

I know how difficult starting a food journal can be, so I have created a food journal you can use at the back of this book.

With this starter keto toolkit, you'll be in the right position to confidently start your keto journey. Your toolkit is your companion on your journey, here to help you when you need it, so make good use of it!

Setting Realistic Goals and Expectations

FIXING YOUR RELATIONSHIP with food will not happen overnight. Your journey won't be smooth, and your days will be up and down. And let me tell you...

That's OK! It's NORMAL.

Putting pressure on yourself to *perfectly* start the keto lifestyle straight away or to suddenly stop emotionally eating the moment your body enters ketosis is unrealistic. Your body and mind are going through a big change, unlearning old behaviours and replacing them with more helpful ones. So here are five important things to do to set realistic goals and expectations for your keto lifestyle journey.

1. Forgive yourself for emotionally eating

MOST PEOPLE WHO EMOTIONALLY eat feel guilty about it. You might feel frustrated and out of control, blaming yourself for your eating. But all that does is put you in a negative shame spiral and make you more likely to continue comfort eating as a way to self-soothe.

You don't need to feel ashamed of your emotional eating. Comfort eating was your way of coping with difficult feelings at a time when you didn't have the tools and resources you needed to deal with your emotions in a different way. Emotional eating was you doing the best you could in that moment. **So forgive yourself for it.**

Now you're cultivating the tools and resources to evolve from emotional eating and deal with your mental wellbeing in a different way. You're changing the way you eat. You're finding healthy ways to address your emotional needs, such as finding connection, building your self-confidence and seeking therapy. And while your unconscious mind is catching up to these new resources, you might still experience the occasional emotional eating session. Forgive yourself for it and move on with your new lifestyle. You're learning and evolving. It takes time.

2. Start as slowly as you need to

MANY PEOPLE THINK THAT as soon as you decide to embark on a keto lifestyle, you immediately need to aim for ketosis. After all, reaping the benefits of ketosis is why you're doing this, right?

But rushing into it is a surefire way to fail and give up before you start. It's like trying to run a marathon without training or expecting to score 100% on a Greek exam when you've never even heard the language before.

It's OK to slowly start adapting your diet day by day, week by week. Let's say your current macronutrient breakdown is 60% carbs, 30% fat and 10% protein. It's nowhere near a keto macronutrient ratio, and dropping your carbohydrate intake from 60% to 10% overnight is completely unsustainable for most people, especially if you have an unhealthy relationship with food.

Instead, spend a week or two eating a macronutrient balance of 50% carbohydrates, 40% fats and 10% protein. Once you're used to it, and it feels second nature, switch it up again, this time to 40% carbohydrates, 45% fats and 15% proteins. Keep doing this until you reach the macronutrient breakdown needed for ketosis (approximately 10% carbohydrates, 70% fat and 20% protein).

This is just a rough guide to how you can slowly change your diet to reach your optimum level for ketosis. Listen to your own body and make the moves that feel right for you. If that means going slower, go slower. If it means going slightly quicker, do that.

The important thing is not to shock your system and make it feel unsafe. That's when you're most at risk of emotional eating.

3. Focus on building an abundance mentality

HOW YOU VIEW YOUR EATING habits and the foods you eat will directly affect how likely you are to keep up with them.

When looking at the keto diet, most people focus on everything they are "giving up." They have to remove carbohydrates, sweets and sugary snacks from their diet. This is an unhelpful way to approach keto as it triggers what's known as "the last supper" mentality. You may already have experienced it yourself. It's a common practice in diet culture where, before starting a new diet, you have a full-on feast of every "bad' (not in keeping with your new diet) food because you believe it's the last time you'll ever eat it. But more often than not, it makes you feel sick and even harder to follow an eating plan.

As I mentioned at the beginning of this book, keto isn't a diet; it's a lifestyle. To make it sustainable, focus on everything you'll be adding to your dishes instead of what you're taking away from the plate. Get excited about avocados, cloud bread, roast chicken, and all the yummy things you'll be eating.

The more you focus on abundance and what you add, the less likely you are to give up or trigger your emotional eating habits.

4. Have an emotional support team in place

HAVING PEOPLE TO TALK to when you're going through a big change is essential for your wellbeing. Whether it's friends, family or support groups online, make sure you find a safe place to talk when you need it.

Your journal is also a safe place to work through your feelings when you don't have access to other people. Getting your thoughts out of your head and into the world, whether through speaking or on paper, takes away some of their power and stops you from feeling trapped and ruled by them.

5. Don't give up on yourself

PROGRESS ISN'T AN UPHILL trek; it's a winding path that goes up, down and all around. One day, you'll feel on top of the world; the next you may feel like you can't do it anymore.

It's important to remember that, as with all emotions, going through low patches is normal*. So, if it feels hard, don't give up on yourself. Your bad days are just as much a sign of progress as good ones.

Trust your body. Stop what you're doing if something feels wrong and contact your GP. While pushing past your mental barriers is important, it's equally important to listen to your body's cues.

Chapter 4: Keto-friendly Comfort Foods

Satisfying Cravings without Guilt

There are some people who believe food is only for sustenance, nothing else. But they're wrong! Food plays an important part in our social and emotional health too! It's the glue with which we strengthen social bonds and the nectar which makes life sweeter. Food is about more than just keeping your body functioning optimally. Which is why it's OK to indulge in your cravings without guilt.

Some people struggling with emotional eating may have an uneasy relationship with cravings. When you've spent a considerable amount of time using food as a coping mechanism, you start to mistrust yourself around food. Especially when you first begin your recovery from emotional eating. You believe that every craving is a panic sign leading straight to a relapse. In reality, cravings are a completely normal part of eating, and satisfying your cravings every now and then is important to avoid having a binge eating episode down the road. And yes, you can definitely satisfy your cravings while following the keto lifestyle.

The best way to satisfy your cravings is to find the foods you love within the keto spectrum and have them for special occasions, like eating with loved ones. Some of my favourite keto comfort foods include keto chimichangas, cauliflower mac and cheese, and keto cheesecake. **I've added these recipes, plus a few other delicious keto comfort food recipes, at the end of this book.** Try them out and see what you enjoy. These are also great dishes to cook for friends and family to help them see how exciting keto food can be!

Mindful Eating Techniques for Emotional Satisfaction

YOU MAY HAVE HEARD of mindfulness before as a type of meditation, but it can also be used to help improve your relationship with food.

It's a way of staying connected with your eating habits from when you enter the grocery shop until you've eaten the last bite on your plate. As such, it's an extremely powerful tool in battling comfort eating and really simple to do too!

In Chapter 5, I'm going to give you a list of powerful mindful eating exercises you can do that will help you stay present and reduce the likelihood of emotional eating.

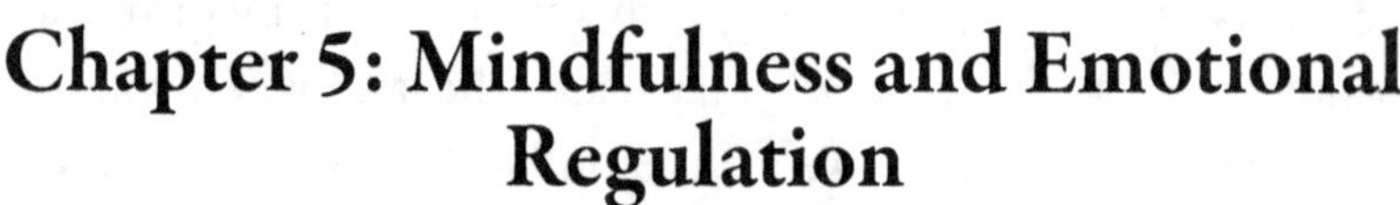

Chapter 5: Mindfulness and Emotional Regulation

The Power of Mindful Eating

You may already be aware of the benefits of mindfulness as a way of dealing with stress and anxiety. As we touched on earlier in this book, these are common emotions that cause comfort eating. So it makes sense that adopting mindfulness in your eating practice can help reduce your comfort eating, too.

When you eat mindfully, you eat with intention, savouring every mouthful and respecting your food's journey to get to your plate. You'll also become more aware of your emotions and, as a result, start to recognise when your emotions are dictating your hunger. This will allow you to step back and assess if eating is the right action right now or if opting for a different coping strategy to address your emotional needs would be more helpful.

If you're unsure how to eat mindfully, here are a few suggestions you can do by yourself, with friends or with your family.

The Mindful Shopping Trip

BEING MINDFUL WHEN eating starts from the moment you step into the supermarket (or open your grocery app). When picking your food, think of the journey it's taken to get to your hands. Has it come from overseas? Has it gone through multiple processes to take its current form? How does the food you're holding make you feel?

Ideally, a mindful eating approach involves consuming whole or minimally processed foods that haven't had to travel long or far to reach your home. But if money makes it harder for you to follow this mindful approach, remember that with food, the goal is always to buy the best food you can afford. As long as you take the time to appreciate and acknowledge where your food comes from and how it makes you feel, you're already on your way to a mindful eating approach.

The Raisin Exercise: Taste, Touch, Smell

THIS METHOD, CREATED by Jon Kabat Zinn, is about appreciating the food on your plate. It's split into eight actions to take when eating. While it may seem excessive, the idea is that by going through the motions now, you'll create the subconscious habit of mindful eating in the future.

The eight steps are:

Holding: Hold the food in your hand. What do you notice about it? Is it light or heavy?

Seeing: Look closely at your food. Notice every line and how the light reflects off of it...

Touching: How does it feel between your fingers?

Smelling: What does it smell like?

Placing: Put the food in your mouth, but don't chew yet. Move it around your mouth, noticing how it feels.

Tasting: Now, you can start chewing. What is the taste profile? What are the textures like as you bite into it?

Swallowing: Follow your food as it goes down your throat, feeling it move.

Following: Is there an aftertaste? Do you have the urge to go for another bite? Are you satisfied?

You don't have to do this for every bite of food you eat, but the more you practice this. The more you'll habitually start mindfully eating.

Zero Distractions Dining

A LOT OF TIMES, WE eat lunch in front of a screen. Be it the TV, a phone screen or having a quick lunch at the work desk. The problem is eating when distracted causes us to miss vital hunger and satisfaction cues that lead to overeating and not enjoying our meals.

It is also an opportunity to tune into our emotional cues. If you feel uneasy, anxious, bored, or any other extreme emotion, you may find you're not hungry but need to regulate your emotions healthier (such as journaling, taking a walk or talking to someone). This kind of introspection is hard to do when you're sat in front of a screen.

Some people find it uncomfortable to eat alone in silence, and it isn't always possible to find someone to eat with at every meal. But even if it feels uncomfortable at first, you'll find your relationship with food improves thanks to it. Plus, if you're using Jon Kabat Zinn's raisin test above, you'll have plenty to keep you interested throughout your meal!

Strategies for Emotional Regulation

ALL THE MINDFULNESS exercises above are excellent at making you more aware of your eating habits and regaining control over what you eat. But there may be days when your emotions are running particularly high, and you can't get your brain to focus on mindfulness.

If that happens, here are a few extra ways you can regulate your emotions so you can better incorporate mindful eating into your daily routine.

4-7-8 breathing

BREATHING IS ONE OF the most powerful tools in emotional regulation. While it seems overly simple, it works. The increase in oxygen to the brain helps with mental clarity, while the focus on your breath helps reduce blood pressure, in turn reducing the feeling of stress and anxiety in the body.

4-7-8 breathing is easy. Breathe in for four seconds. Hold it for seven seconds. Then, breathe out for 8 seconds. Do it for as long as you need to calm down. Why not give it a try now and see how you feel?

Manage your sleep

YOU MAY HAVE OUTGROWN your childhood bedtime, but it's time to impose a new one. Sleep is how our body and mind repair themselves; without sufficient sleep, everything suffers. There are plenty of reasons you might not be getting enough sleep, but insomnia, caffeine and bedtime procrastination are the most common among people struggling with their mental health and emotions.

While sticking to a bedtime may not come naturally, it will allow your body the time it needs to repair, helping you better regulate your emotions in the long term.

Get active

BEING ACTIVE IS THE last thing you want to do when you're having a rough day. But it's also one of the best ways to *stop* your bad day before it worsens.

Being active doesn't have to mean hitting the gym. It can be doing housework, dancing, stretching, running around with your pets — anything that gets your blood pumping. Any movement is going to help release feel-good endorphins and improve your mood.

Combining Keto with Mindfulness

STARTING YOUR KETO journey is the perfect excuse to pair it with mindfulness. Given the nature of this eating plan, you'll need to be more mindful of the foods you're eating anyway, especially as it pertains to macronutrient content. So, it makes sense to take this observation a step further by coupling it with a more holistic, mindful approach.

Think about the new tastes you're exploring and how they make you feel. Acknowledge the journey your food has taken to get to your plate. Make mealtimes a family affair and spend your time socialising instead of staring mindlessly at the TV screen.

It can also help you better understand and differentiate your hunger cues. Studies show it takes approximately 15 minutes to signal your brain after your stomach is full. By eating mindfully, you'll be eating slower, giving your brain plenty of time to assess your fullness levels and stop any overeating caused by trying to prevent emotional hunger feelings in the stomach.

Embarking on the keto lifestyle is the perfect opportunity to start being more present. To start being more proactive in your eating habits. So make sure mindfulness is a big part of your keto journey.

Chapter 6: Overcoming Challenges

Dining with Friends and Family: Balancing Social and Keto

Eating is even more enjoyable when shared with the people you love. Keto can feel isolating at times, especially when most people you're dining with have a higher carbohydrate intake than you can allow for in your keto diet. But that shouldn't deter you from dining with friends and family.

Here are a few different ways you can easily dine with your friends and family without having to sacrifice your keto diet.

1. Host a dinner party

SHOW YOUR FRIENDS AND family how great the keto lifestyle can be by cooking for them. When you host a dinner party, you're in control of the food options, meaning you'll always have something you can eat. And your loved ones will see just how delicious mealtime can be, even with very few carbs on the plate!

2. Hook your loved ones up with some delicious keto recipes to try

GET YOUR FAMILY AND friends involved with your new lifestyle by sharing some of your favourite recipes with them. Not only will this help them understand your journey a bit more, but it will also give them options when you eat at their house.

You can even make it a fun afternoon together, cooking and having fun trying all your favourite keto recipes and seeing how your loved ones like them.

3. Take or make your own meals

IN AN IDEAL WORLD, you would be catered for everywhere you go. But there may be times when no keto options are available (or at least none you particularly like). To get past this obstacle, if you know there is unlikely to be any food you can eat, just make your own and bring it along! If it's a buffet, no one will even notice. And if you're headed to a sit-down dinner, give your host a waning so they aren't offended (they won't be, though!).

4. Find keto-friendly restaurants you can all enjoy

EATING IN WITH FRIENDS and family is easy, but eating out can be a bit more difficult. A lot of popular restaurants serve particularly carb-heavy dishes (think pasta, pizza, bread, rice, battered foods...). This limits the options of restaurants you can go to where everyone will enjoy something from the menu. Do your research before going out and present your friends with a few options of friendly places you'd love to visit, and let them see if there's anything on the menu they like. By having options in advance, you're almost guaranteed to find a great dining option everyone can enjoy.

Taming Plateaus: Keeping Your Keto Fire Burning

IF YOU'RE USING KETO for fat loss, you may experience a weight plateau at some point on your journey. Typically, this happens two to four months after you first enter ketosis, and it's a pretty common obstacle to cross.

There are a few reasons why you might hit a plateau:

- Slow metabolism
- Not enough protein
- Eating inflammatory foods
- Eating too many calories
- Not eating enough calories
- Taking certain medications that cause weight gain as a side effect
- Stress causing an increase in cortisol levels
- Sleep disturbance
- Emotional eating

Hitting that plateau can feel incredibly demoralising, especially after all your progress. The instinct most people have is to throw in the towel. To believe you've done all you can do and it just won't happen for you anymore.

But plateaus aren't the end. They're like a comma in the middle of a sentence. A short pause before normal service resumes.

Now is the time to re-evaluate your keto lifestyle. To double-check your macros, pay attention to the food quality, address any potential food intolerances you may have, and ensure you're building muscle to keep your metabolism up.

You may be stuck at a plateau for a while, but keep making small changes to address it, employ a little trial and error, and most importantly, don't look back. Think of all the incredible, non-scale victories you're still having, like feeling satisfied, having more energy, and better mental wellbeing. You've come too far to throw in the towel now.

Bouncing Back from Emotional Lapses

JUST LIKE HITTING A plateau, you may find yourself reverting back to emotional eating on particularly trying days. You must understand that one comfort eating session does not undo your progress.

The whole purpose of this book is to teach you how to find food freedom. But food freedom isn't a fixed target; it's a lifelong process. And if you've spent many years of your life in the habit of comfort eating, it will take many months, maybe even years, to kick the habit for good.

It takes a delicate mixture of addressing your emotional needs, finding joy in different activities and managing your relationship with food through keto to help you down the path to freedom.

So, if you find yourself at the end of a comfort eating session, find the strength to be kind to yourself. Appreciate the food you ate, remind yourself that sometimes your brain reverts back to your old ways, but it's learning every day not to, and remember that you can't change the past, but you **can** change the future.

Take a deep breath and continue as usual. There's no need for course correction; you're already doing great. A relapse or two every so often is not a cause for concern — it's a part of the process.

Chapter 7: Success Stories and Testimonials

Real-life Accounts of Comfort Eaters Who Found Freedom in Keto

I cannot talk enough about how powerful the keto lifestyle is in not only achieving better health but also finding freedom from your emotional eating. But sometimes, you need to hear it from other people for the message to really sink in. People who were once where you stand today and who have worked hard to make it through to the other side.

So, after struggling with emotional eating for most of their lives, I reached out to a few people who were finally able to break the chains of comfort eating using keto.

Here's what they had to say...

Lauren P, 45 years old:

"COMFORT EATING WAS my coping mechanism, especially during times of stress or emotional turmoil. This habit was wreaking havoc on my health and self-esteem. I needed change. Turning 45 was a wake-up call for me. I realised that I needed a change, not just to shed the extra weight but to break free from the toxic relationship I had with food. That's when I discovered the keto diet, and it completely transformed my life. The cravings for sugary, comforting junk food vanished. Cravings were replaced by energy and satisfaction from satisfying, high-fat foods. Clothes fit better, but more importantly, my mood lifted, I have more consistent energy and I no longer have the guilt that comes with emotional eating. Today, I'm happier and healthier than ever. Keto changed not just my body but my whole outlook on life. If you're struggling, give it a shot. It's not just a diet; it's a path to understanding yourself, your triggers and controlling your emotional eating habits."

Irene W, 50 years old:

"AS I ENTERED MY FIFTIES, managing my weight and hormones felt like an uphill battle I'd never win. I had all but given up hope. But then, the keto diet came into my life, and it's been nothing short of a game-changer. I found the balance I thought was lost forever. Following the keto lifestyle not only helped me regain control of my weight but also regulated my emotions in a way I hadn't experienced in years. My cravings diminished, my energy surged, and the stubborn weight began to melt away. I felt like myself again! But it wasn't just about the weight. The keto diet brought emotional stability. Hormone fluctuations that once drove me crazy were now manageable. The rollercoaster of mood swings became a thing of the past. At 50, I've found a new lease on life, and it's all thanks to the keto diet. If you're in a similar place, I encourage you to give it a try. It's never too late to take back control of your body and your emotions."

Ash McL, 47 years old:

"I'D STRUGGLED FOR YEARS with comfort eating. My journey to regain control started with the understanding that comfort eating was a psychological response triggered by stress. It was the first step toward healing. Recognising the triggers and patterns allowed me to confront them head-on. The missing piece of the puzzle came when I discovered the keto diet. Keto not only helped me shed the weight, but it also rewired my relationship with food. A sense of calm and control replaced the cravings that once sent me spiralling. I've reclaimed my life. Stress triggers are no longer a signal to overindulge; they are a call to physical and mental self-care."

Jess, 35 years old:

"BEING A MOM OF YOUNG children is beautiful, but it can also be a whirlwind. Somewhere along the way, I struggled with weight and turned to comfort eating whenever life got a little too chaotic. It took me a while to realise that it wasn't just about the food. There was a deeper psychological aspect to my eating habits. Understanding the triggers, the emotional responses, and the patterns was my first big step towards change. When I found keto, it wasn't just a diet but a new way of life. It wasn't about depriving myself; it was about nourishing myself. The high-fat, low-carb approach helped me shed unwanted weight and brought a sense of balance and control. No more drowning emotions in a bag of chips. No more guilt trips after a late-night fridge raid. Keto became my ally in this journey towards a healthier, happier version of myself."

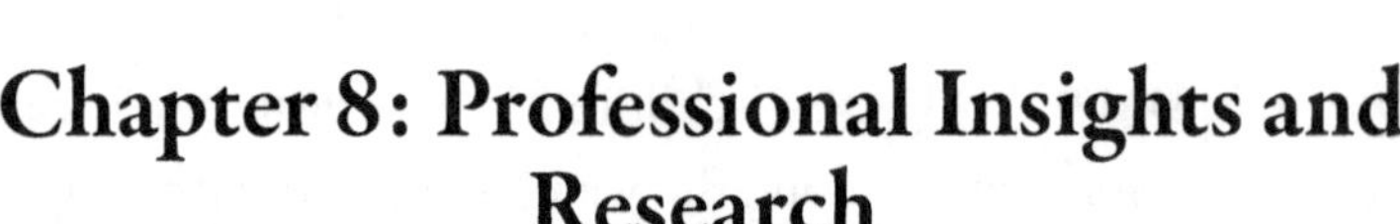

Chapter 8: Professional Insights and Research

Interview with an Eating Disorder Specialist Psychologist

One of the best professional insights I've ever seen into emotional eating was from an online interview by Dr Julie T. Anné, a clinical psychologist with 27 years of experience specialising in eating disorders. In the interview, she discusses everything from why people comfort eat to the meaningful steps we can all take to overcome emotional eating.

Her answer stood out to me when asked why people comfort eat.

"Emotional comfort eating is a behaviour characterised by using food as a means to cope with negative emotions. It's imperative to recognise that this is distinct from physical hunger; **it's the hunger of the heart and mind,**"

She then explained how emotions such as stress, loneliness, boredom, sadness, and sometimes even elation can cause us to reach for our favourite comfort food snack. And every time we do that, we're strengthening the connection between our emotions and the need to eat, leading us to use food to deal with our feelings.

So how can we change that?

According to Dr Anné, the most powerful first step is to start a food journal so you can start understanding your triggers. As she puts it, "This exercise can be instrumental in identifying recurring patterns and pinpointing the emotions that instigate your compulsion to eat emotionally." In this way, you might find out you habitually reach for the biscuit tin when you're stressed at work or cook up a hearty batch of mac and cheese when you're feeling bored or alone. Understanding these triggers empowers you to take a proactive stance in addressing them.

Dr Anné, like myself, is also a big believer in the power of mindfulness to break the cycle of emotional eating. She agrees that "Mindfulness can heighten your awareness of your emotions as they surface, allowing you to respond to them more constructively."

Dealing with comfort eating alone is hard. Dr Anné suggests that if your emotional eating has become persistent or distressing, you should reach out to a mental health professional. "A therapist can guide you in delving into the root causes of your emotional eating, forging healthier coping strategies, and nurturing a more positive relationship with food."

Emotional eating is tough, but when you find the triggers, you empower yourself to start making meaningful changes in your life. With mindfulness, self-awareness and professional support, the journey to food freedom is possible.

Listen to the full interview here[1].

Scientific Studies on Keto and Emotional Eating

THERE ARE SOME PROMISING studies on the effects of following a ketogenic lifestyle on eating behaviour. While most studies are done on binge eating disorder (a more severe, clinical diagnosis that emotional eating can lead to), due to the similar nature of BED and comfort eating, it is likely that what works for binge eating will also work for emotional eating.

A 12-week study by Morhoko et al. (2018) followed 35 overweight participants to see how the diet changed their eating behaviour, cognitive function and physical benefits. At the end of the study, participants reported significant weight loss, improved physical performance, better blood sugar levels, a reduction in appetite, improved body image satisfaction and, most importantly, a significant decrease in the frequency of emotional eating. A separate case study by Carmen et al.

---

1.   *https://www.weightmanagementpsychology.com.au/drjulietanne/*

(2020) found that a low carbohydrate keto diet can be used successfully as a treatment for food addiction and BED.

A study on people following keto who have type 1 diabetes and suffer from eating disorders by Schneider et al. (2022) found that thanks to the metabolic effects of ketosis, including the improvement in blood sugar levels, symptoms of eating disorders, including binge eating disorder, significantly decreased. The idea that blood sugar levels have a significant impact on the likelihood of eating disorders and disordered eating is backed up by a study on the connection between diabetes and eating disorders by K. Ismail (2008).

In a study on women following a very low-calorie ketogenic diet for 21 weeks as a way to treat BED, by Rostanzo et al. (2021), participants reported no binge eating by the end of the study. However, it's important to note this could also be due to the removal of highly processed junk food from their diet, highlighting the importance of opting for minimally processed foods. In fact, in a review by Ayton and Ibrahim (2020), they discussed the idea that most comfort and binge foods are ultra-processed, which affects blood sugar levels, messes with our hormones and stimulates appetite. This could help explain how the foods we comfort eat lock us into a negative cycle and supports the idea that following a minimally processed keto diet can help break this cycle.

Finally, we are aware of the underlying psychological mechanisms behind emotional eating, such as anxiety, stress, and depression. A study by Norwitz et al. (2020) found that such mental illnesses could be improved by following the keto diet, as ketosis allows more glucose into the bloodstream for brain function and slows down or stops glucose hypometabolism.

Chapter 9: Long-Term Sustainability

Transitioning to a Balanced Lifestyle

Once you've been doing keto for a year or two, you'll start learning what works for you and what doesn't. You'll have a better understanding of your emotional eating triggers, the foods that make you feel satisfied and full of energy, and you'll have a toolkit full of mental health and keto go-to's to help you on your way.

As you become more confident in your knowledge and abilities, keto becomes second nature. You'll have plenty of tricks to make keto living as easy and stress-free as possible.

You'll start recognising your emotional triggers more efficiently and be able to intercept them with activities that benefit you mentally and physically.

The key to making keto part of your balanced lifestyle is to reconnect with the reason you started to begin with and the benefits you've gained along the way.

And remember, balance is all about listening to what feels best for your mind and body. So if one day you eat a couple more carbs, or you decide a soft keto diet is more suitable, go for it! The most important thing is you feel great inside and out!

Preventing Relapses

AN EMOTIONAL EATING session every once in a while isn't a cause for concern. We've already discussed why your mind may revert to this in times of high stress.

However, if you find yourself emotionally eating more and more often, you may be on the path to relapse.

First things first. Don't panic.

There are plenty of ways you can intervene before you end up fully relapsing.

1. Analyse your thoughts

USE YOUR FOOD DIARY to pay attention to any emerging patterns so you can find healthier ways to regulate your emotions. It may be that you've entered a particularly stressful time at work, you may be going through hormonal imbalances, or there may be some things going on in your personal life triggering your anxiety. Recognising what's bringing you back to emotional eating is the first step to stopping a relapse.

2. Make a plan

KETO TAKES A LOT OF planning in the beginning as you become acquainted with a new way of eating, paying attention to macronutrients, which is something you may never have done before.

3. Seek professional help

YOU DON'T HAVE TO DO this alone. If you're struggling, please get in touch with a mental health professional or your GP. Sometimes, we all need help, and your medical professional can give you tailored solutions to suit your specific emotional needs.

Finding Joy Beyond Comfort Eating

PART OF OVERCOMING comfort eating is finding better and healthier habits that bring you a sense of joy, peace and serenity. The kinds of activities you can do when you feel that dreaded sense of anxiety in the pit of your stomach and your mind starts blaring the comfort food siren.

There's no one way to find joy beyond comfort eating, but through trial and error, you can create a mental well-being toolbox with a list of go-to activities that make you feel great.

Here are some examples of activities you can try to replace your comfort eating habit with:

- Go for a walk
- Practice mindfulness
- Call a loved one
- Meet up with friends
- Do some stretching
- Put on a funny show and laugh

Put these ideas, and any more you come up with, in your keto toolkit, ready to pull out when you feel like you might emotionally eat.

Conclusion

Empowering Comfort Eaters: You Can Break Free

THE COMFORT EATING habit of a lifetime may feel impossible to break. It's not. You have everything you need to start to understand your emotional needs so you can stop relying on food for comfort.

I've said it before, and I'll say it again. This journey isn't an easy one. But, the fact you've reached the end of this book should be more than enough encouragement that you're ready to start dealing with your emotional needs.

You know that this journey will take time, but all journeys do. Take it one day at a time, go slowly and allow yourself to make mistakes. When you do, you'll find the grip comfort eating has on you becomes looser every day.

Don't worry about getting it right the first time. Just keep putting one foot in front of the other, and everything will fall into place.

The Journey Ahead: Continuing the Path of Self-Discovery

THIS JOURNEY YOU'VE started is an empowering one. You're about to unlock your emotional and mental blocks and learn new coping mechanisms that will enhance your life.

Overcoming comfort eating is the goal, but the introspection you'll be doing on your journey will lead you down some interesting roads.

You're about to learn a lot about yourself. Lean into the adventure and enjoy the journey. In a year, you may just find yourself somewhere you never thought you could be. When you learn to accept your emotions and regulate them healthily, there's no stopping you!

References

1. Appleton, J. (2018). The Gut-Brain Axis: Influence of Microbiota on Mood and Mental Health. *Integrative Medicine: A Clinician's Journal*, 17(4), 28-32. https://www.ncbi.nlm.nih.gov/pmc/articles/PMC6469458/

2. Agnes Ayton, Ali Ibrahim, The Western diet: a blind spot of eating disorder research?—a narrative review and recommendations for treatment and research, *Nutrition Reviews*, Volume 78, Issue 7, July 2020, Pages 579–596, https://doi.org/10.1093/nutrit/nuz089

3. Awad, G., Befort, K., Olmstead, M.C. (2021). Artificial Sweeteners in Animal Models of Binge Eating. In: Avena, N.M. (eds) Animal Models of Eating Disorders. *Neuromethods*, vol 161. Humana, New York, NY. https://doi.org/10.1007/978-1-0716-0924-8_7

4. Carmen, M., Safer, D.L., Saslow, L.R. et al. Treating binge

eating and food addiction symptoms with low-carbohydrate Ketogenic diets: a case series. *J Eat Disord* **8**, 2 (2020). https://doi.org/10.1186/s40337-020-0278-7

5. Godet, A., Fortier, A., Bannier, E. et al. Interactions between emotions and eating behaviors: Main issues, neuroimaging contributions, and innovative preventive or corrective strategies. *Rev Endocr Metab Disord* 23, 807–831 (2022). https://doi.org/10.1007/s11154-021-09700-x

6. Ismail, K. (2008). Eating disorders and diabetes. *Psychiatry*, 7(4), 179-182. https://doi.org/10.1016/j.mppsy.2008.02.006

7. Macht, M. (2008). How emotions affect eating: A five-way model. *Appetite*, 50(1), 1-11. https://doi.org/10.1016/j.appet.2007.07.002

8. Marlicz, W., Misera, A., Koulaouzidis, A., & Łoniewski, I. (2018). Microbiome—The Missing Link in the Gut-Brain Axis: Focus on Its Role in Gastrointestinal and Mental Health. *Journal of Clinical Medicine*, 7(12), 521. https://doi.org/10.3390/jcm7120521

9. Mohorko, N., Černelič-Bizjak, M., Poklar-Vatovec, T., Grom, G., Kenig, S., Petelin, A., & Jenko-Pražnikar, Z. (2019). Weight loss, improved physical performance, cognitive function, eating behavior, and metabolic profile in a 12-week ketogenic diet in obese adults. *Nutrition Research*, 62, 64-77. https://doi.org/10.1016/j.nutres.2018.11.007

10. Norwitz, Nicholas G.a; Sethi, Shebanib; Palmer, Christopher M.c. Ketogenic diet as a metabolic treatment for mental illness. *Current Opinion in Endocrinology & Diabetes and Obesity* 27(5):p 269-274, October 2020. | DOI: 10.1097/MED.0000000000000564

11. Rostanzo, E., Marchetti, M., Casini, I., & Aloisi, A. M. (2021). Very-Low-Calorie Ketogenic Diet: A Potential Treatment for Binge Eating and Food Addiction Symptoms in Women. A

Pilot Study. *International Journal of Environmental Research and Public Health*, 18(23), 12802. https://doi.org/10.3390/ijerph182312802

12. Schneider, E., Biggerstaff, D., & Barbe, T. (2022). Helpful or harmful? The impact of the ketogenic diet on eating disorder outcomes in type 1 diabetes mellitus, *Expert Review of Endocrinology & Metabolism*, 17:4, 319-331, DOI: 10.1080/17446651.2022.2089112[1]

13. Timmerman GM, Acton GJ. The relationship between basic need satisfaction and emotional eating. *Issues Ment Health Nurs.* 2001 Oct-Nov;22(7):691-701. doi: 10.1080/016128401750434482. PMID: 11881182.

14. Van Strien, T., Gibson, E. L., Baños, R., Cebolla, A., & Winkens, L. H. (2019). Is comfort food actually comforting for emotional eaters? A (moderated) mediation analysis. *Physiology & Behavior*, 211, 112671. https://doi.org/10.1016/j.physbeh.2019.112671

15. Harvard Health Publishing. (2018, October 18). What is "Keto flu"? [Webpage]. *Harvard Health Blog*. https://www.health.harvard.edu/blog/what-is-keto-flu-2018101815052

16. Melissa Spann. (2022, March 30). Emotional Eating and Binge Eating Disorder. *Rosewood Ranch*. https://www.rosewoodranch.com/emotional-eating-and-binge-eating-disorder/[2]

17. Anné, J. (2019, July 31). Stop self-sabotage and end binge eating (Episode 4) [Audio podcast episode]. *The Glenn Mackintosh Show - A Health Psychology Podcast*. Glenn Mackintosh. https://www.weightmanagementpsychology.com.au/

---

1. https://doi.org/10.1080/17446651.2022.2089112

2. https://www.rosewoodranch.com/emotional-eating-and-binge-eating-disorder/

drjulietanne[3]

Appendices

Your Self-Assessment Quizzes

Questionnaire 1: Stress and Emotional Triggers

1. Do you find yourself reaching for comfort foods when you are stressed, anxious, or overwhelmed?
2. Have you noticed a pattern of emotional eating during specific situations or events, such as work deadlines, family conflicts, or relationship issues?
3. When you experience emotional distress, do you tend to eat large quantities of food quickly, even when you're not physically hungry?
4. Do you use food as a way to distract yourself from uncomfortable emotions or memories?
5. Have you ever tried to soothe feelings of sadness, loneliness, or boredom with food?

Questionnaire 2: Social and Environmental Triggers

1. Do you eat more than usual in social situations, such as parties, gatherings, or celebrations, even when you're not hungry?
2. Are there specific people or places that trigger your comfort eating, such as certain family members, friends, or environments?
3. Do you feel pressure to eat certain foods or specific amounts of food when dining out with others?
4. Have you ever used food as a way to fit in or conform to social

---

3. https://www.weightmanagementpsychology.com.au/drjulietanne

norms?

Questionnaire 3: Body Image and Self-Esteem

1. Do you find yourself eating to cope with negative thoughts or feelings about your body image?
2. Have you ever used food as a reward for achieving weight-related goals or to punish yourself for not meeting them?
3. Do you feel guilt or shame after eating certain foods, even in moderation?
4. Have you ever engaged in restrictive diets followed by episodes of overeating or binge eating?

Questionnaire 4: Loneliness and Relationship Triggers

1. Do you eat to fill a void when you feel lonely or disconnected from others?
2. Have you noticed that your eating habits change in response to relationship issues or conflicts?
3. Do you use food as a way to seek comfort or solace when you're experiencing difficulties in your personal life or romantic relationships?
4. Have you ever felt that food is your primary source of emotional support?

Questionnaire 5: Boredom and Routine Triggers

1. Do you often eat out of boredom or as a way to break up the monotony of your daily routine?
2. Are there certain times of the day when you're more likely to engage in mindless snacking, even when you're not hungry?
3. Have you ever found yourself eating while watching TV,

browsing the internet, or engaging in other distracting activities?

4. Do you use food as a way to make routine tasks more enjoyable?

Recipe Ideas for Keto Comfort Foods

Banana Pancakes

THIS RECIPE MAKES: 6 Servings
Prep Time: 5 Minutes Cook
Time: 10 Minutes
Total Time: 15 Minutes
Ingredients:

- 2 large free-range eggs
- 1 banana
- 1 tablespoon almond flour

Serve with:

- 50g full-fat yoghurt
- 1/2 teaspoon cinnamon

Instructions:

1. In a bowl, mash the banana. In another bowl whisk the eggs.

2. Combine the eggs, mashed banana and almond meal and form the batter – there should be no lumps. If it's too thick, add a splash of water.

3. In a non-stick frying pan over medium-low heat, pour in a portion of your batter (this should make 4-6 pancakes in total). After about 2 minutes, the top of the pancake should start to form bubbles and dry.

Flip and cook for a further minute. Depending on your frying pan, you may need a dash of oil to prevent sticking.

4. Divide the pancakes between two plates, then top with yoghurt, banana slices, and a sprinkle of cinnamon.

Nutritional Information (per serving):
Calories: 469
Protein: 32.7g
Fiber: 10.5g
Carbs: 25.1g Fat: 24.6g

Crispy Low-Carb Parmesan Almond Crackers

THIS RECIPE MAKES:: 5 Servings
Prep Time: 5 Minutes
Cook Time: 20 Minutes
Total Time: 25 Minutes
Ingredients:

- 65g sliced almonds, lightly crushed
- 145g shredded parmesan cheese

Instructions:
1. Preheat the oven to 170°C. Line a baking tray with parchment paper.

2. Spread half of the parmesan cheese onto the prepared pan.

3. Evenly sprinkle the gently crushed, sliced almonds over the cheese.

4. Layer the remaining cheese over the almonds.

5. Use your hands to push any stray bits into the rectangle, forming an even edge.

6. Bake for 10 minutes (the cheese will be bubbly and melting).

7. Remove from the oven. Allow the crackers to rest for about 30 seconds.

8. Using a pizza cutter, slice the dough first lengthwise, then width-wise. Typically, 4 cuts lengthwise and 8 cuts width-wise result in 45 individual crackers. Gently separate each cracker.

9. Return to the oven for 7-10 minutes until the crackers begin to turn golden. Remove from the oven. Place the crackers on a cooling rack for 10 minutes, and they will crisp as they cool.

Nutrition Information (per serving):

Calories: 194

Total Fat: 14.3g

Total Carbohydrates: 3.8g

Fiber: 1.5g

Sugar: 1.6g

Protein: 13g

Cauliflower Mac and Cheese

THIS RECIPE SERVES: 6

Prep Time: 20 Minutes

Total Time: 1 Hour 20 Minutes

Ingredients:

- Butter, for baking dish
- 2 medium heads cauliflower, cut into florets
- 2 tablespoons extra-virgin olive oil
- Kosher salt
- 1 cup heavy cream
- 170g cream cheese, cut into cubes
- 500g shredded cheddar
- 250g shredded mozzarella
- Freshly ground black pepper

For the Topping:

- 114g bacon – diced and fried
- 30g freshly grated parmesan
- 1 tablespoon extra-virgin olive oil
- 2 tablespoons freshly chopped parsley, for garnish

Instructions:

1. Preheat the oven to 190°C and butter a 22 cm x 33 cm baking dish.

2. In a large bowl, toss cauliflower with 2 tablespoons of oil and season with salt. Spread the cauliflower onto two large baking sheets and roast until tender and lightly golden, about 40 minutes.

3. Meanwhile, in a large pot over medium heat, heat the cream. Bring it up to a simmer, then decrease the heat to low and stir in the cheeses until melted. Remove from heat and season with salt and pepper.

4. Fold in the roasted cauliflower. Taste and season more if needed.

5. Transfer the mixture to the prepared baking dish.

6. In a medium bowl, stir to combine bacon bits, parmesan, and oil. Sprinkle the mixture in an even layer over the cauliflower and cheese.

7. Bake until golden, about 15 minutes. If desired, turn the oven to broil to toast the topping further, for about 2 minutes. Garnish with parsley before serving.

Nutrition Information (per serving):

Calories: 650

Fat: 56g

Saturated Fat: 30g

Trans Fat: 1g

Cholesterol: 165mg

Sodium: 791mg

Carbohydrates: 8g

Fiber: 3g

Sugar: 5g

Protein: 29g

Keto Chimichangas

THIS RECIPE MAKES: 6 Servings
    Prep Time: 10 Minutes
    Cook Time: 15 Minutes
    Total Time: 25 Minutes
    Ingredients:

- 6 low-carb tortillas
- 500g minced beef
- 2 tablespoons taco seasoning
- 90g salsa
- 250g shredded cheese
- 2 tablespoons butter or coconut oil
- 250ml red enchilada sauce
- 500ml sour cream
- Fresh red chillis - chopped
- Fresh green shallots – chopped

Instructions:

1. Cook off the minced beef. Add the taco seasoning.
2. To each tortilla, spoon 60g of taco-seasoned meat, 2 tablespoons of salsa, and 2 tablespoons of shredded cheese down the centre. Fold in the sides and wrap into a burrito.
3. In a frying pan over medium heat, melt the butter. Add the burritos and pan fry for 30-60 seconds on all sides, until browned and slightly crispy. You may have to do this in batches.
4. Transfer the burritos to an oven-safe pan or dish. Top each with 2 to 3 tablespoons of enchilada sauce and the remaining shredded cheese.
5. Bake in the oven at 180°C for about 8 to 10 minutes until the

cheese is melted.

6. Serve with sour cream and sprinkle some chopped chillis and shallots on top.

Nutrition Information (per serving):
Calories: 418
Total Fat: 26.2g
Total Carbohydrates: 24.7g
Fibre: 16.7g
Sugar: 2.3g
Protein: 33.3g
Net Carbs: 8g

Keto Cheesecake

THIS RECIPE MAKES: 1 cheesecake
Prep Time: 5 minutes
Cook Time: 40 minutes
Total Time: 45 minutes
Ingredients:
For the Crust:

- 315g keto cookie crumbs (or whole cookies if you can't find ready-made crumbs)

- 80g butter (melted)

For the Cheesecake Filling:

- 500ml cream cheese, softened and at room temperature
- 160ml sour cream, room temperature
- 3 large eggs, room temperature
- 90g superfine sugar substitute (erythritol)
- 1 tablespoon vanilla extract

Instructions:
1. Preheat the oven to 160°C. Line a 9-inch springform pan with parchment paper or tin foil and set aside.

2. In a high-speed blender, add your keto cookies and blend until a fine consistency. Measure out 315g and place it into a mixing bowl. Add the melted butter and mix together until combined.

3. Transfer the cookie crust to the lined springform pan and use the back of a spoon to spread it around the edges. Refrigerate the crust while you prepare the filling.

4. In a high-speed blender or food processor, add the cream cheese, sour cream, and superfine sugar substitute, and blend until combined. Add the eggs, then the vanilla extract, and blend once more until fully incorporated.

5. Remove the pie crust from the refrigerator and add the cheesecake filling to it.

6. Place the cheesecake in the oven and bake for an hour, or until the middle is mostly set.

7. Turn off the oven and open the oven door slightly. Allow the cheesecake to cool in it completely before refrigerating for at least four hours to firm up.

Nutrition Information (per serving):
Calories: 192
Carbohydrates: 6g
Protein: 5g
Fat: 19g
Sodium: 309mg
Potassium: 154mg
Fiber: 3g
Net Carbs: 3g

Keto food and recipe resources

KETO FOOD LIST[4]

Keto food blogs:

KETO CONNECT[5]
Keto in Pearls[6]
Ketogasm[7]

---

4. https://www.womenshealthmag.com/weight-loss/a23494478/keto-diet-grocery-list/

5. https://www.ketoconnect.net/

6.   https://ketoinpearls.com/

Little Pine Kitchen[8]
The Keto Queens[9]
The Primitive Palate[10]
Cast Iron Keto[11]
Meat Free Keto[12]

---

7.   https://ketogasm.com/

8.   https://www.thelittlepine.com/

9.   https://theketoqueens.com/

10.   https://theprimitivepalate.com/

11.   https://www.castironketo.net/

12.   https://meatfreeketo.com/